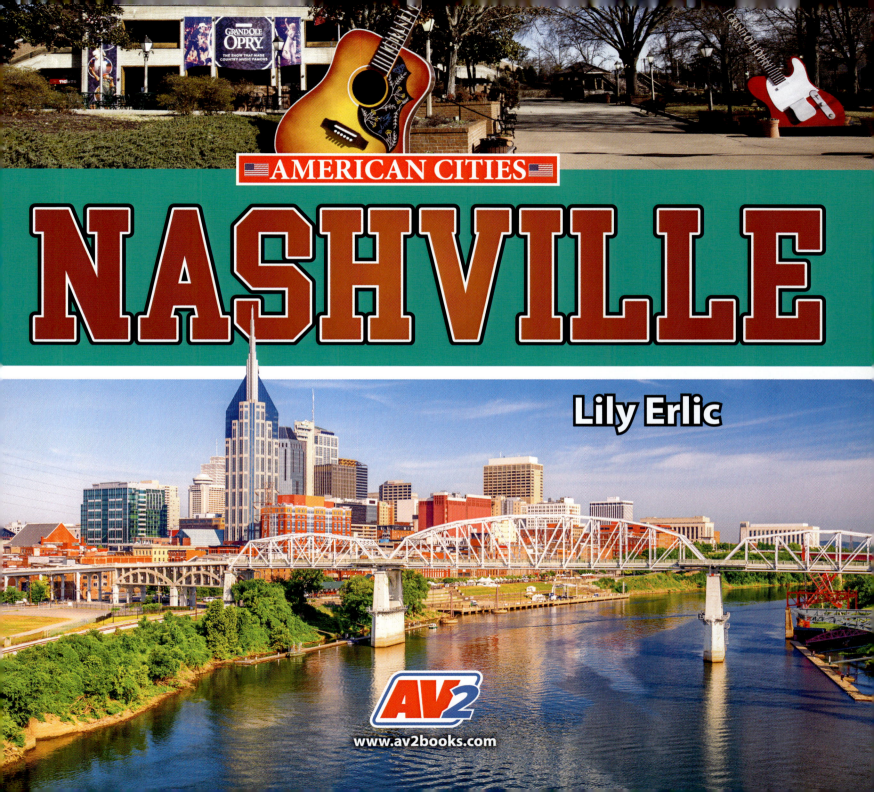

AMERICAN CITIES
NASHVILLE

Lily Erlic

Step 1
Go to www.av2books.com

Step 2
Enter this unique code
COVFMRUK1

Step 3
Explore your interactive eBook!

Your interactive eBook comes with...

AV2 is optimized for use on any device

Audio
Listen to the entire book read aloud

Videos
Watch informative video clips

Weblinks
Gain additional information for research

Try This!
Complete activities and hands-on experiments

Key Words
Study vocabulary, and complete a matching word activity

Quizzes
Test your knowledge

Slideshows
View images and captions

View new titles and product videos at www.av2books.com

Contents

- 2   AV2 Book Code
- 4   Get to Know Nashville
- 6   Where Is Nashville?
- 8   Climate
- 10 Population and Geography
- 12 Many Peoples
- 14 Tourism
- 16 Sports
- 18 Economy
- 20 Nashville Timeline
- 22 Things to Do in Nashville
- 24 Key Words

Get to Know Nashville

Nashville is the capital city of Tennessee. It is also the state's largest city. Nashville is sometimes called "Music City." This is because it is the home of country music. The Country Music Hall of Fame is found here.

Where Is Nashville?

Nashville is in north-central Tennessee. It is 212 miles from Tennessee's second largest city, Memphis. You can travel to Memphis from Nashville by going southwest on the I-40 highway.

There are many other exciting places to visit in Tennessee. You can use a road map to plan a trip. Which roads could you take from Nashville to get to these other places? How long might it take you to get to each place?

TRAVELING TENNESSEE
Nashville to Wynnewood State Historical Site 38 miles
Nashville to Fall Creek Falls State Park 108 miles
Nashville to Knoxville 180 miles
Nashville to Cherokee National Forest 246 miles

Climate

Summers in Nashville are hot and humid. Winters are cool and mild. The city can have snow in the winter. Rain falls mostly in the spring. Fall is dry, but cool.

Nashville can have extreme weather. Thunderstorms often take place in the spring and summer. They sometimes bring tornadoes with them. These strong winds can harm people and buildings.

In **1998**, Nashville had **2 tornadoes** in **1 day**.

Population and Geography

Nashville is home to almost 700,000 people. Another 1.75 million people live in the area around the city. Only about one quarter of these people are under 18 years of age.

Nashville was built on the banks of the Cumberland River. This river runs through the city's downtown. Many events are held on and along the river every year.

Many Peoples

Aboriginal Peoples were the first people to live in the Nashville area. Fur traders arrived in about 1717. They set up a trading post.

In 1779, a group of settlers came to the area. They cleared the land and built farms there. They also built a fort. The settlers called their new home "Fort Nashborough." The name was changed to "Nashville" in 1784.

In 1800, only **300 people** lived in Nashville.

Tourism

Most people visit Nashville to hear country music. Some of the world's best-known artists perform there. The Grand Ole Opry and the Ryman Auditorium both hold concerts throughout the year.

Nashville is also known for its Parthenon. This building is a copy of a temple in Greece. Nashville's Parthenon is an art museum.

Nashville's Parthenon features a **42-foot statue** of a Greek goddess named Athena.

Sports

Nashville has two major sports teams. The Tennessee Titans are the state's football team. They play in the National Football League. Their home field is Nashville's Nissan Stadium.

The Nashville Predators play ice hockey for the city. They belong to the National Hockey League. Their home games take place at Bridgestone Arena.

Economy

Tourism is important to Nashville's economy. More than 14 million people visit the city every year. They spend money on hotels, food, and events.

The city is also known as a center for health care. More than 500 health care companies call Nashville home. They provide jobs for about 270,000 people in the city.

In 2018, Nashville was the city with the **4th strongest** economy in the United States.

Nashville Timeline

12,000 years ago
Aboriginal Peoples live in the Nashville area.

1779
Fort Nashborough is built.

1806
Nashville becomes a city.

1826
The University of Nashville is founded. It closes in 1909.

1843
Nashville becomes the permanent capital of Tennessee.

1933
A tornado hits downtown Nashville, damaging the State Capitol.

1961
The Country Music Hall of Fame is founded.

2018
Nashville is named one of the best places to live in the United States.

Things to Do in Nashville

Nashville Zoo
More than 2,700 animals from all over the world live at this zoo. Visitors are welcome to pet a kangaroo, touch a tortoise's shell, or brush a goat.

Nashville Children's Theatre
This theater has been hosting plays for children since 1931. It is the oldest professional children's theater in the United States.

Adventure Science Center

This science center offers visitors 175 hands-on adventures. People can find out what it is like to be weightless in space or go back in time to see the dinosaurs that once roamed the land.

The Hermitage

The Hermitage was home to Andrew Jackson, the country's seventh president. Its site contains more than 30 historic buildings, including the 13-room mansion.

State Capitol

The Capitol is perched on the highest hill in downtown Nashville. Free tours offer visitors a chance to learn more about the history of the building.

KEY WORDS

Research has shown that as much as 65 percent of all written material published in English is made up of 300 words. These 300 words cannot be taught using pictures or learned by sounding them out. They must be recognized by sight. This book contains 117 common sight words to help young readers improve their reading fluency and comprehension. This book also teaches young readers several important content words, such as proper nouns. These words are paired with pictures to aid in learning and improve understanding.

Page	Sight Words First Appearance
4	get, know, to
5	also, because, city, found, here, home, is, it, of, sometimes, state, the, this
7	a, are, by, can, could, each, from, how, in, long, many, might, miles, on, other, places, take, there, these, use, where, which, you
8	and, but, day, had, have, often, people, them, they, with
11	about, almost, along, another, around, every, live, one, only, river, runs, through, under, was, years
12	came, changed, farms, first, group, land, name, new, set, their, up, were
15	an, both, for, hear, its, most, some, world
16	at, has, play, two
19	as, call, food, important, more, than
20	closes
22	all, animals, been, children, do, or, over, things
23	back, be, country, find, go, hands, learn, like, once, out, see, that, time, what

Page	Content Words First Appearance
4	Nashville
5	Country Music Hall of Fame, music, Tennessee
7	highway, map, Memphis, roads, trip
8	buildings, climate, damage, fall, rain, snow, spring, summers, thunderstorms, tornadoes, weather, winds, winters
11	age, area, banks, Cumberland River, downtown, events, geography, population
12	Aboriginal Peoples, fort, Fort Nashborough, fur traders, settlers, trading post
15	artists, art museum, Athena, concerts, copy, goddess, Grand Ole Opry, Greece, Parthenon, Ryman Auditorium, statue, temple, tourism
16	Bridgestone Arena, field, football, games, ice hockey, Nashville Predators, National Football League, National Hockey League, Nissan Stadium, sports, teams, Tennessee Titans
19	center, companies, economy, health care, hotels, jobs, money, United States
20	timeline, University of Nashville
21	State Capitol
22	goat, kangaroo, Nashville Children's Theatre, Nashville Zoo, shell, visitors
23	Adventure Science Center, Andrew Jackson, chance, dinosaurs, hill, history, mansion, president, site, space, The Hermitage, tours

Published by AV2
350 5th Avenue, 59th Floor   New York, NY   10118
Website: www.av2books.com

Copyright ©2021 AV2
All rights reserved. No part of this publication may be reproduced, stored in a retrieval system, or transmitted in any form or by any means, electronic, mechanical, photocopying, recording, or otherwise, without the prior written permission of the publisher.

Library of Congress Control Number: 2019039079

ISBN 978-1-7911-1594-4 (hardcover)
ISBN 978-1-7911-1595-1 (softcover)
ISBN 978-1-7911-1596-8 (multi-user eBook)
ISBN 978-1-7911-1597-5 (single-user eBook)

Printed in Guangzhou, China
1 2 3 4 5 6 7 8 9 0   24 23 22 21 20

012020
100919

Project Coordinator: Heather Kissock   Designer: Ana María Vidal

AV2 acknowledges Getty Images, Alamy, Shutterstock, and iStock as the primary image suppliers for this title.
Page 22B: Michael Scott Evans.